DREAM 4 REAL

Mariana Leader

To my special littles ones, Emma and Luca,
for their own special big dreams

CONTENTS

INTRODUCTION FOR YOUR PARENTS

I remember the first time I read about goals, why it is important to set them up and write them down, and the power within ourselves to make our dreams a reality. I would love to tell you I was just a child, a teenager or even a young adult, but the reality was that I had already changed careers several times, had already moved to another country, had already tried and failed many times to find myself. I was already in the wrong side of my thirties! Yes, I know. Some of you may think it was already too late for me to get into this train, that it had already departed, and Silly Me was still waiting by the station. On the contrary, learning about goal setting gave me the possibility of making some of my dreams a reality in just a few years: I travelled around the world from the Americas to the Far East and all that is in between, I earned a bachelor degree with honours, I started my own business, I learned two more languages to make a total of four, I got a fabulous condo in a high rise and my dream car, I spoke in front of hundreds of people for Fortune 100 companies around the world, I helped the most unfortunate people when they needed parenting, financial, and career advice and I mentored kids and teenagers.

After reading about me, I am positive you can see why not only

I became an advocate, but the biggest fan of goal setting. I am obsessed with learning about it, developing new goals, and creating plans to make them a reality. I love to hear about other people's dreams and motivations. I find it truly inspiring to share my ambitions with my friends and family, and it energises me when I can support and encourage others to make their dreams come true. I am passionate about living the best life I can and inspiring others to do the same.

What am I doing with my life at this moment? I am married to the love of my life, and we have the sweetest, most beautiful kids in the world (well, I know you also have the best kids, so can you blame me if I think mine are?). As soon as my kids were born, I had the desire, will, responsibility and obligation to teach them about the ways to create their ideal life. That moment finally arrived, and I wrote this book with that purpose in mind: to help my children understand the power of their own determination, and how they can plan, set up, and have the best life they can ever imagine.

To accomplish this (new) goal, I have written this book directly for them, with some guidance for them to use as support when creating their goals, and then some pages written as a workbook, with questions and exercises that will help them discover their passions and dreams. The first part of the book is an introduction to discovery: your kid will learn who they are, what they are good at and what they want to improve, and then who they want to become, and how they can make it happen by setting up goals. The second part will immerse them in the creation of their goals, starting from dreams and progressing to SMART goals. Then they will learn about how to create a plan to achieve each goal and how to overcome challenges and setbacks. Finally, we will talk about support and habits, so they have all the resources they need to succeed.

I hope I can help you empower your own kids to create the life they want, so you can also make their dreams come true.

INTRODUCTION
FOR YOU

Emma is nine years old and is in year four. She loves her friends, her toys, going to school, and attending her other activities: swimming, art, cheerleading, and dance. But she still does not know what she wants to be when she grows up. Sometimes she thinks she wants to be an artist, other times a scientist, and yet other times a teacher. "It doesn't matter yet, Emma," I say to her when she talks about her confusion. "You are young; you still have time to decide." But I do remember being nine years old and looking forward to being an adult and becoming whatever I wanted. Time went by and when it was time for me to go to university, I still didn't know what career I wanted to study because I still didn't know what I wanted to be.

You may relate to Emma. I am sure you love your friends and your family, your toys and your school, your sports and whatever you do for fun. What would you think if I told you that your life can always be full of this amount of fun? What would you think if I told you that all your dreams can become a reality and that it is all within your control? That you have the power to be whatever you want to be, do whatever you want to do, and have whatever you want to have? You can dream as high as you want, as far as you want, as immediate as you want. Do you think we need a fairy godmother to make those dreams come true? Or perhaps a magic lamp out of which a genie can come to hear our wishes? How about a rainbow, with a unicorn on top to bring us to the other side where all the dreams have come true? No, we don't need any of that. We can leave the fairy godmothers, the genies, and the unicorns on rainbows inside beautiful books. All we need is a little imagination, a little planning, and some hard work to follow that plan. As a result, you will see all your dreams can become reality. Let's go dreaming and have some fun!

PART 1

Foundation

In these chapters, we will learn all about goals, what they are, their difference to dreams, why it is so important to create them, and how this book can help you create them, plan them, and look for ways to make them a reality. It is very important that you read this part of the book because it will help you understand what you can achieve by creating your goals and how to use this book to imagine the most amazing life you want to have. This is where you will find the energy, the push, the emotion that you will need to keep you going when you are working for your dreams. Yes, there is some work to do. But if you imagine the dreams that really matter to you and properly plan what you need to do to make them a reality, then that work will not feel like a chore (or like Maths!). It will feel like a breeze! That is why these first few chapters in this part of the book are very important. I am sure you will love them!

CHAPTER 1: WHAT ARE GOALS?

Who has not heard about the Matildas nowadays? This group of girls that are some of the best soccer players in the world have made a name for themselves in the World Cup. One reason is that they score more goals than many other teams. You could believe there are no similarities between the goals that the Matildas score with what we are talking about in this book. But think about it: the Matildas work really hard every day of every week of every month to play good soccer and score some goals. They think about scoring goals every minute they are awake, and maybe even dream about it while they sleep! Their focus is on scoring as many goals as possible so they can win every game they play. That is why they are superstars!

If you compare the way the Matildas score goals, it looks very similar to the way you can realise your dreams: you think about them constantly, you may even dream about them. You focus and concentrate on making your dreams a reality, and you must work really hard on the activities you need to complete to achieve your dreams. And that is why from now on we will start calling your dreams "goals." Because "dreams" or "wishes" rarely become reality. Usually only fairies or genies in a bottle can grant dreams and wishes. But the idea is not to hope that at some point in our life a fairy or a genie will appear magically to make our dreams come true, because if we wait for them, we will end up waiting forever. Instead, it is better (and more realistic) if we are in control and decide, create, and work on making our own dreams a reality, and score big goals in life!

The fun thing about deciding what our goals will be is that we can choose whatever we want them to be. We can decide that we want to become a teacher, a policeman, or an astronaut. We can decide that we want to save money to buy the biggest Barbie dollhouse or the coolest bike we can find. We can decide we want to win the STEM contest or even be part of the Matildas team! So, as you can see, all the imagination that you have, the one that helps you create stories to play with your dolls and robots, the one that helps you build large cities or beautiful ice cream shops with your LEGO®, is the same one that will help you create, develop and plan the dreams you want to come true. And then make them come true!

Learning how to create goals when you are still a kid will allow you to get used to planning the best life you can have now and not having to wait until you are an adult. It is possible to start making your life dreams a reality while you are still in school. It is important to create goals you like and care about, and that are in tune with your likes and interests. Do not think your goals won't matter just because you are a kid. Those goals matter more than anything! Because by creating your goals when you are young, you will practise how to make your dreams come true even for small things. And in the meantime, you will have more fun seeing how anything you want to do, have or be becomes a reality.

On the other hand, you must be thinking: how am I going to make my dreams come true if I am just a school kid with no super-powers? The reality is that you already have in you what it takes to make your dreams come true whenever you want, without having to wait for something or someone else to do it for you. What do you think is better: to wait for a genie or superpowers (forever) or to live the life you want (now)? Instead of waiting forever, you already have all the materials, ingredients, and resources you need to make your dreams come true:

Materials for Creating and Making Dreams Come True:

1. 10 kg of imagination to create the best dreams you can.
2. 5 kg of energy to work really hard on them.
3. As much determination as you need to never give up
4. Infinite happiness to enjoy the dream come true.

You can see how you do not need a lot for it to happen, just your willingness to achieve your goals, and a good plan of action that you can follow, so you can do, be or have whatever you want. And I will show you in this book through some reading, some thinking, and some writing, how you can do it yourself.

CHAPTER 2: WHO AM I?

O ne of the most important things we have to do to create good goals is to know a lot about ourselves: our likes, our interests, our talents, and also our dislikes, what is boring or uncool for us, and what we are not so good at, even if we do not care about improving it (for example, I am definitely not good at cricket, but I am really not interested in it and do not feel it is important for me to improve my game!). That is exactly what we will do on this chapter: we will learn more about ourselves so we can recognise and understand what goals are important for us to achieve, and what resources we can count on to achieve such goals.

The first thing we look at is our talents. What are we really good at? What do people usually say that is so good about us? Because you are so good at something, most probably you would also like and be very interested in it. However, try not to focus on what you like or are interested in, but just on what you are good at and what good qualities you have. In a moment you will need that pen to complete the answers to the questions below, which will help you think more in depth about your talents and qualities.

One point you must consider is how and what you will answer.

It is super important that you answer the questions thinking only about yourself. Because these questions are very personal, you should not think about what your parents, teachers, or friends tell you or what you think they would like to hear from you. The reality is that you know yourself better than anybody else, so you will know better than anybody what to answer. Another thing you may think is that you "must" write the right answer. You may start thinking about changing your answers for something that you think would be right. I have good news for you: this is not a test. (Awesome!) Nobody will examine your answers, and nobody can tell you what would be correct or incorrect. (Happy face.) In this book there are no right or wrong answers. This is your book, this is your life, these are your goals. All you have to do is be honest with yourself and answer with the truth, your truth.

Exercise 1: Activities I love

Think about all the activities you do or attend throughout the year. Which ones do you enjoy the most? Circle between three and five. If you love an activity that does not appear in the list, feel free to add it below the chart.

Swimming	Soccer	Painting and sketching
Reading	Maths	Rugby
Tennis	Basketball	Any sport
Ballet	Dancing	Lego
Roblox	Fashion design	Cheerleading
Chess	Singing	Writing stories
Playing the guitar	Playing the piano	Athletics
Cooking	Surfing	Crafts
Knitting and sewing	Science and robotics	Going to the museum
Travelling	Gardening	Drama and theatre
Riding a bike	Skating	Skiing
Photography	Boy Scouts/Girl Guides	Public speaking
Babysitting younger kids	Yoga	Learning a language
Martial arts	Golf	Gymnastics
Horse riding	Cricket	Pottery and sculpting

Exercise 2: Activities I am good at

In this exercise you will see the same activities. This time you need to circle the ones you think you are good at, even if you do not like them as much. Circle between three and five. If you are really good at an activity that does not appear in the list, feel free to add it below the chart.

Swimming	Soccer	Painting and sketching
Reading	Maths	Rugby
Tennis	Basketball	Any sport
Ballet	Dancing	Lego
Roblox	Fashion design	Cheerleading
Chess	Singing	Writing stories
Playing the guitar	Playing the piano	Athletics
Cooking	Surfing	Crafts
Knitting and sewing	Science and robotics	Going to the museum
Travelling	Gardening	Drama and theatre
Riding a bike	Skating	Skiing
Photography	Boy Scouts/Girl Guides	Public speaking
Babysitting younger kids	Yoga	Learning a language
Martial arts	Golf	Gymnastics
Horse riding	Cricket	Pottery and sculpting

Now that you completed the first two exercises, look at both lists. Do you see that you have chosen the same activities in both exercises? It is very probable that you have, mostly because we tend to enjoy what we are good at. But it also may happen that you like something you cannot do well yet. For example, you may really like athletics, but every school carnival you end up last in every competition. It does not matter at all. We can all improve everything we put our minds to, and if you really like an activity and you set your mind to it, you can improve your performance. Think about the best athletes and sports people in the world: they got to become number one not because they were born that way but because they practised almost all day every day.

On the other hand, you may be superb at something but not particularly enjoy it. For example, I know many kids that are incredibly talented mathematicians, but they don't want to spend all day with numbers.

If you are still unsure about what activities you fancy more, or what you are talented at, how about you go around and ask your parents, your grandparents, your teachers, and your friends, to see if they can recognise some of your talents and qualities? Sometimes we may find it a bit difficult to pinpoint some of our own characteristics, but people that know us and love us the most could give us a hand.

Exercise 3: My Achievements

To dig deeper into all your talents and strengths, think about what you have achieved so far in your life. You may think you are still too young to have achieved much. But if you think harder, in these short years you have already achieved a lot! For example, didn't you learn how to walk and talk? Didn't you learn how to read and write? Perhaps you bake the best brownies in the family, or perhaps you won a trophy in soccer. Think of every situation when you were proud of yourself and succeeded, no matter how young you were. I will show you a few examples for you to use as inspiration, and then you can fill in the blanks. If you need extra space, you can complete the exercise in a notepad.

- Won a trophy for soccer.

- Got a merit certificate for mathematics.

- Learned to speak Mandarin Chinese.

- Came second place in the spelling bee at school.

- Won a race at the school swimming carnival.

- Got recognition for a STEM project.

- ....

- ....

- ....

- ....

- ....

- ....

- ....

- ....

Exercise 4: My Qualities

During this exercise think about your talents. What are some of your good traits? Circle ten of the qualities in this list you believe represent you.

Empathetic	Supportive	Accepting
Sympathetic	Easygoing	Resilient
Funny	Curious	Sociable
Intelligent	Assertive	Respectful
Creative	Polite	Responsible
Brave	Friendly	Patient
Fearless	Determined	Passionate
Humble	Honest	Adventurous
Fair	Self-confident	Compassionate
Optimistic	Grateful	Thoughtful
Helpful	Caring	Generous
Trustworthy	Forgiving	Affectionate
Joyful	Hardworking	Perseverant

Exercise 5: My Weaknesses

This final exercise will give you some idea of what you want to work on for yourself, and what you don't. The idea here is to think about your weaknesses, what you are not so talented in, or what qualities you wish you had. Writing them down will help you recognise areas of improvement that you could work on through your goals. It may also help you recognise some lack of resources in your own personality that may make it difficult or inconvenient to achieve a certain goal. Don't worry about this part so much yet. We will learn at the end of the book how to overcome setbacks or challenges in our process to achieve goals. The same way as in the previous exercise, you will see a few examples to give you some idea of what to think about, and then there will be some space for you to write. If you need extra space, you can complete the exercise in a notepad.

- I am not good at athletics.
- I am a bit slow when I get ready for school.
- My swimming stroke is not correct.
- I am too shy.
- I get too distracted in school.
- ....
- ....
- ....
- ....
- ....
- ....

Excellent job completing your first set of exercises! These exercises help you understand who you are, what you are good at and what goals you would be more motivated to choose. They will guide you on what strengths you can count on as resources to achieve your most important goals.

Considering that after all this thinking you know what you are good at, what you are not good at, and what you can accomplish, let's start with what you need to create those dreams and wishes, and how to transform them in actual goals. This way you will make them a reality.

PART 2

Creation

This is the fun part. Here you will have the possibility to use your imagination as much as you want, so you can think of the most beautiful dreams and wonderful wishes you would like to become a reality. We will learn how to create a structure that is solid enough for the dream to be realised, so that the dreams will become goals, just because those dreams and wishes will have a structure to bring them to real life, and a plan to make this possible. I know it sounds like a lot, and you must be thinking, "Where do I start? This is too much!" But do not worry; as I did in the previous chapters, I will explain what you will think about before creating your goals and how you will create them. You will also need a pen to write answers to certain questions and exercises that will inspire you and help you create the best goals for yourself and will motivate you to make them happen. To the Dream Headquarters!!

CHAPTER 3: WHAT KIND OF DREAMS WILL I CREATE?

Whenever you think of dreams and wishes, you may think of having superpowers, or being able to fly, or having all the toys in the world. Let's be honest, those dreams are really not possible to make a reality, right? Not just that, but imagining only that kind of dream will rob you from thinking about a lot of other dreams that may also be important for you and you may also want to accomplish. The best way to have all the most important dreams you can think of and imagine is to start with a structure. Think about it as "boxes" where you put all your dreams in different sections, depending on what the dreams are about. Let me explain this concept so you can see how good it will be for the creation of your dreams.

I remember the first time I arranged my children's (Emma and Luca) toys in different drawers. Emma's drawers included one for Barbies, one for Barbie's accessories and clothes, one for LOL Surprise dolls, one for Shopkins and one for dress-ups. Luca's drawers were: one for trucks and cars, one for blocks, and one for his teddies. And then there were drawers that both were interested in, like the one for musical instruments, the one for Playdough® and the one for LEGO®. The first time we placed all the toys in each drawer, the kids thought it was a big task that did not have much benefit for them. But now that they have their toys divided into each section, they can see how much easier and more convenient it is. Every time they think about playing a certain game or doing an activity, they do not need to spend time going through all their toys looking for the ones that they want. Not only that, they also know right away if they need more Playdough® or if they are missing a particular toy.

We will use that same idea to imagine all our dreams and create our goals. First, we must think of all the categories we will use to create each goal, and then we will start dreaming. That way you know you are considering all the important aspects of your life, which will help you create the best goals that will keep you motivated through each of the steps in your plan.

So how can you think of the different "drawers" or "boxes" you want to create before we create the goals? You must think of everything important to you. For example, your family is something that is very important for you because you love them so very much and you want the best for them, and to always be by their side. On the other hand, you may consider sports to be something especially important in your life as well. Or your toys, because how much fun it is playing with all that LEGO®, right? You can even think of what you would like to be when you grow up. Let's say you want to be an artist, so art would be a very important part of your life as well. Let's think about it in our next exercise.

Exercise 6: What is important for me?

Write every aspect of your life that you find it important for you. As in the previous exercises, you will find some examples to inspire you and some blank space for you to use.

- Family

- Friends

- School

- Sports

- Art

- Toys

- ....

- ....

- ....

- ....

After having selected the categories you find most important, let's see what goals you will create for each of them. You can think of any kind of goals you want. You can also create as many goals as you like for each of them. But something that you must consider is how much priority each category has in your life. This is particularly important because sometimes we don't have the time to pursue all our dreams. If we want to be sure we will achieve something, we must be sure that we will have the time to dedicate to work on that something. If you create too many goals, or even just one goal for each category, you may feel overwhelmed, or you may feel that you are spreading yourself too thin and by no means will you be able to achieve everything. If that happens, you are at risk of not doing anything, giving up completely, and feeling even worse than when you had no goals at all and no desires. We are going to prioritise each category in the next exercise.

Exercise 7: Establishing Priorities

Next to each category you created, put a number, from 1 being the most important aspect of your life and what you want to dedicate the most time to when pursuing your goals, to the last number being more of a "like" or "would be great if but not super necessary." When you finish, copy each category, organising them in order from the most to the least important. Having this structure organised this way will allow you to visualise better where you will spend most of your time and energy. Below you will find the list with numbers for you to complete with your own prioritised categories list:

1. ....

2. ....

3. ....

4. ....

5. ....

6. ....

7. ....

8. ....

9. ....

10. ....

Now that you have the list of categories in front of you, take a little time to read them through. Do they truly stand for what you consider the most important aspects of your life? Does each of them represent the path where you want to spend the most time and energy? Will you feel energised, passionate, and motivated when you work on each of those categories? What happens if you answer "no" to one or all those questions? Then peace out! Gone!

If you feel that one (or several) of them does not totally represent what you (and only you) want, please take it off. Delete it. Do not feel guilty about it. Remember, no teacher or parent or anybody will grade or judge you on these exercises, so there is no right or wrong answer. Also, since only you will be the one working on each goal, there is no reason to create a category that will please other people but not yourself. Finally, if you only want to work on one category instead of many, please do so, and only leave one, your most important one, the one that brings you the most joy, on the list. This is very important because in the next chapter we will start creating the goals, so you need to be confident about the kind of goals you want to work on. Great job!

CHAPTER 4: IT'S TIME TO BE SMART!

The moment to dream like there is no tomorrow has finally come. You now have in your mind a ticket to Dreamland and all it requires you to do is dream. So put your imagination hat on, do not hold back, and let's spend this exciting time "sketching" how you see your life will end up being in the future. What are you going to achieve? What will you have? What are you going to make? How will you behave? This is fun! Actually, the whole process is fun, but this is the part where you get to think about what does and will make you happy.

Reading the title of the chapter, it might feel confusing for you how being SMART relates to dreaming. "I thought there is no silly, or right, or wrong when you are dreaming," I bet you are thinking. However, the word SMART is not about how silly, right or wrong you or your dreams are (which they are not). It defines the structure used to describe your dreams, to transform them into actual goals that you will be able to achieve. That is how your dreams will become possible and you will be able to make them a reality. This may sound difficult to do, because we usually think of dreams as something impossible or unobtainable. So, you may be thinking, "How can I transform something impossible into something possible?" Don't worry, the SMART process will allow you to do that. Like any process, this one also has steps, so let's start from the beginning and look at each step one at a time and in order. That process is what the word SMART stands for:

S	Specific
M	Measurable
A	Achievable
R	Relevant
T	Timely

Let's explore each of the words and what they mean for you in the goal creation process:

S – Specific

I am sure that so many of your dreams sound specific enough. You may want to excel at your favourite sport, or at school, or have lots of toys. But just saying that is not enough, because those goals are not specific. To make those dreams a reality and create a specific goal, you must continually ask yourself exactly WHAT you want to achieve or get. For example, my daughter Emma is excellent at swimming, and she enjoys it very much. So, her dream could be to be the best swimmer, but that would not be specific enough because she would not know when she becomes the best. To make that dream more specific, she could modify her goal and rewrite it to winning her upcoming school swimming carnival. If your dream is to excel at school, your specific goal could be to get to the next level up in all your classes. Or if you want to have new toys, your specific goal could be to save $20 of your pocket money to buy the latest LOL Surprise Doll. In short, when you think about a specific goal, you must think about what exactly it is that you want to happen. The more detailed you are, the more chances for you to achieve your goal.

M – Measurable

If you want to know if you have achieved your goal, then you will have to state it in a way that will be obvious to recognise. If your goal is to be a better student, how do you know if you achieve it or not? You could decide that your goal is to reach the next level in your spelling lists. Then you would know without a doubt when you achieve that goal: at the moment that you move up one level in your spelling lists. Another example would be "saving money" versus "saving $25." Just saving money is not measurable because it does not tell you if you achieved it or not. Like you could have found a 5 cent coin in the street and put it in your pocket, so there you go, you achieved your goal, right? Nope. The idea is to know exactly when you reached your goal.

A – Achievable

This is the part where we bring those crazy dreams back to real life. If your dream is to have a unicorn, then that is something not achievable because they don't exist (what? You didn't know? Oops, sorry) then you could never accomplish that dream. If your dream is to participate in the Olympics next year, that is also impossible, unless you will be 16 years old by the next Olympics and have been training seriously for years. The problem is that if you set up a non-achievable goal, not only it will be a complete waste of time, but you will give up after a while (or after a minute and a half) when you realise that it is extremely hard to make it happen. It is good to be ambitious; you should aim really high! As a matter of fact, it is necessary for the goal to be challenging or you will not feel motivated to work on it, it will bore you to tears, and, worst of all, there will be no improvement if you find it too easy to achieve. But ambitious does not mean crazy! One way to realise if your goal is realistic and achievable is to think of all the steps and actions you would have to take to make it a reality.

Let's see, to have a unicorn, first step: get a horse, second step, glue a horn on his head. Great! Achievable! (Just kidding, I have a little suspicion that no parent would allow that.) Don't overthink this. Just think quickly about what you would have to do to make your dream happen, and you will recognise whether it is achievable or not. If we go back to the example of taking part in the next Olympics, one of the main steps would be to train day and night in a certain sport. Well, that indeed would not make the goal achievable, because you would have to miss school, sleep, playing with your friends, and lots of other activities! Just thinking about it makes me exhausted, and if we are exhausted, we would never have the motivation and energy necessary to accomplish the goal. That is why it is so important that we create goals that are possible to achieve.

R – Relevant

How would you like to be completely selfish and think only about yourself, what you want, what you like, and what you need? This is the way to think if you want your goal to be relevant. A goal is relevant when it is absolutely connected with yourself, your passions, your personality, your own desires – and nobody else's. Sounds like fun, right? Because it is! In the beginning, you may find it a bit difficult not to think about what Mum would like you to do or what Dad what like you to be or how to impress your teacher. But it is very important that you think only about what you really want or like and what you are truly interested in. The reason to think this way is so you know it won't feel like a chore when you are working towards achieving that goal. If you find that one of your goals is something you are not interested in achieving, and was created only because you thought your parents would be proud of you if they knew you were working on such a goal, then when it comes time to work on it, it will feel like a chore, like something you have to do instead of want to do. The result is that it will take you much more energy to complete each step of your plan, and you may not do them right, or it will take you much longer, and at the end you will not be happy. Or you will give it up completely after a short time. Or both.

You may think: "What is the big deal about giving up something I don't care about?" Absolutely no biggie here at all, but only if you give it up before you commit to it. If you find that you start committing to certain goals and then quitting in the middle of the process, it may make you feel like you failed, or like you didn't try hard enough, and that is not a nice feeling at all. And worse, it may make you feel like you cannot achieve any goal. And we both know that is not true! Remember all those accomplishments you listed in the previous chapter? And how about all those strengths and skills you have? You don't want a goal that has nothing to do with you ending up making you forget about all that! So, there you have it: make it relevant, important and significant just for you, and you will feel successful, happy, and a champion!

T – Timely

The last letter for the word SMART is a very useful element to consider when creating your goals. Timely (or time-bound) means assigning a due date to your goal. The question you must answer here is: What date am I supposed to or do I intend to accomplish this goal? Assigning a due date to each goal will give you a time frame so you can focus your efforts on following the steps and actions to make your goal a reality. On the other hand, if you don't have a due date, you will end up leaving the goal to start "someday". And I am sorry, but last time I checked there were seven days of the week: Monday, Tuesday, Wednesday, Thursday, Friday, Saturday and Sunday. I have never known of an eighth day of the week called Someday! The reality is that if you don't have an actual date to refer to as the date to accomplish your goal, you will never start, because there is no urgency, as then it just doesn't matter when you start because it doesn't matter when you finish.

Putting SMART together

The time to create your SMART goals has come, with all the considerations and variables about you at the top of your mind. You will need to ensure that each of the dreams you created are Specific, Measurable, Achievable, Relevant, and Timely. If any of them do not meet all those conditions, it will be very difficult, if not impossible, to achieve your goals. I know it is not easy, but if you take your time and don't rush, you will be able to create SMART goals, in a very smart way.

First, remember to answer the question: "What exactly I am looking to achieve?" and to have some measurement as a way to recognise when you have achieved that goal. Then remember to make it challenging but realistic, something that will push you a bit and will take some effort, but is not impossible. After you have done that, look at the goal and answer, "Do I really care about accomplishing this? Is this goal very important and significant for me?" And when you have all your goals set up that way, go back to them one by one and assign a day for your achievement date. Just remember one point when setting up a target date: this must also be realistic. It cannot be realistic to set up a goal such as "learn to speak Chinese" by tomorrow, because that will not happen, and you are unlikely to start practicing even one word. But learning to speak Chinese is realistic and if it is relevant for you (because you really want to do it), then set up a realistic target date and you will be on the right path to success.

Taking into account the formula to transform your dreams in doable goals, let's complete the following exercise so you have your list of SMART goals ready to execute.

Exercise 8: Creating SMART goals

Grab your list of dreams and work on them one by one, converting each of them to SMART goals. As usual, I will add an example to help you visualise what you should do with your dreams. After the example, you can fill in the blank lines with your own answers.

Example:

Dream: Be the best swimmer

SMART Goal: Win at least one competition in the school Swimming Carnival on 11th November 2020.

Does it meet all the SMART conditions?

Specific: Winning a competition at the next carnival

Measurable: One competition

Achievable: I am good at swimming; I just have to train hard to achieve the goal.

Relevant: Swimming is my favourite sport.

Timely: I will achieve this by 11th November 2020.

Dream 1:...

SMART Goal:..

Does it meet all the SMART conditions?

Specific:..

Measurable: ....

Achievable: ....

Relevant: ....

Timely: ....

Dream 2:...

SMART Goal:..

Does it meet all the SMART conditions?

Specific:..

Measurable: ....

Achievable: ....

Relevant: ....

Timely: ....

Dream 3:...

SMART Goal:..

Does it meet all the SMART conditions?

Specific:……………………………………………………........

Measurable: …………………………………………………....

Achievable: …………………………………………………....

Relevant: ……………………………………………………....

Timely: …………………………………………………….....

You can convert more of your dreams if you want. If you need more space, or want to work on other dreams, just grab your notebook and keep writing, and thinking, and transforming. I just wanted to make you aware of one aspect of creating goals: if the goals are relevant enough, all of them will be important enough for you and you may not know where to start. You may feel over-whelmed and may even decide not to take action on any of them. My suggestion is: look at your list of categories for each dream you created and choose three of them that you feel you want to try and work through. Most probably they will be the first three because they are the highest on the priority list. Then convert them to SMART goals. If by the end of the exercise you still think they are too challenging or will take serious effort to achieve, then select only two, or even one, to work on first. You have many years to make all your dreams a reality. There should be no such pressure that would make you not to want to work on any of them. Believe me, when you get a handle on how to create SMART goals and their action plans, you will be able to work on more than one goal at the same time, if that is what you wish. But in the meantime, get one to three dreams and convert them into goals. I promise, even with just one goal, you will have plenty to do.

PART 3

Making Things Happen

I f everything was about dreaming or wishing, you would be staring at nothing all day, sighing about all the good things that could happen to you. Then you would end up going from daydreaming to actually falling asleep! When would you start working on achieving your goals? Because, let me tell you something very important and that many times we are not aware of: time goes by. I can almost hear you screaming: "What?! Really?!! Duh!! What kind of big, huge, enormous, and super important secret is that? Tick Tock, lady! I have a watch and I know that time goes by!"

Welcome to reality, where life just happens, and we are not aware that the minutes pass, the days go by, the months come and go, and when we least expect it, the year is almost over, Santa is coming, we go on vacation, we start a new school year and the dreams are still there: untouched, undone, and unaccomplished. They are staring at us from our notebooks, waiting for us to work on them, bored to tears. (I like imagining my notebook begging me to open it when I pass by it.) So for your notebook not to be bored to tears, or laughing at the pen because it is still on the shelf, or begging you to open it, you have to start working.

This part will help you create a plan for that kind of work. We need to think of what actions we should complete and what steps we should take before the target date we set up for each goal. We will also talk about what will happen during that time and how we will handle each step and each challenge. The idea is to be well prepared so we can succeed. And then who will laugh at that notebook? You!

CHAPTER 5:
PLANNING WHAT
TO DO

L adies and gentlemen, fasten your seatbelts and roll up your sleeves, because it is time to stop dreaming and start working. Well, you will not actually start working yet. But you will need to put your thinking hat on and do some serious thinking to find out exactly what you will have to do to achieve your goals. And when I say serious thinking, I truly mean it. You will use that pen or pencil so much that by the end of this chapter's exercises, you may need a mini bed to lay your hand on for some rest.

At this time the idea is to create your action plan for each goal so you know exactly what you need to do, all the actions to carry out, the steps to climb, and the milestones to achieve so you are headed in the right direction to achieve your goal or goals. This part is very important because it will give you many benefits. Check them out:

1. You will always know exactly what to do to bring you closer to your goal.

2. You will do this thinking and planning prior to performing each step, which means you can stay in autopilot while you work, without having to second guess yourself or waste time thinking about what to do next.

3. You will have guidance and measurement to let you know if you are on target. At all times you will know if you are going to achieve your goal on time, or if you need to work harder, or if you are falling behind, or even if you are way ahead and may even hit your target much earlier than you thought.

4. You can decide in advance whether to delegate certain steps if possible and necessary. When you delegate, you ask somebody to do something for you. For example, if one of your goals is to read one full book every month, one step in your action plan is to get a few books from a library or a bookstore. By creating this action plan, you could see this is one of the steps and delegate it to your mother. What a simple way to accomplish a step! Just remember, there will be many steps, if not most of them, that you cannot delegate because they are part of the work you must complete or training you have to go through to achieve the goal. Plus, even if you delegate, you need to create the action plan to know exactly what steps you will delegate.

As you can see, there are many benefits of creating an action plan for each goal. But one thing is especially important about an action plan: the action part! It may seem like I am being repetitive and obvious here, but with no action on your part, you can plan as much as you want and create as many and as wonderful goals as you wish, but nothing will become a reality just by thinking about it. At the end of a busy day of working, you don't say, "I am clean because I am thinking of having a shower." And neither can you say, "I will be in the top five in the cheerleader competition because I am thinking about practicing my jumps." It is important to imagine the end goal already achieved. But this would be useless if we don't put an action plan in place and start working every day towards achieving our goal. As Nike says in their advertisement: Just do it!

So in the following exercises you will be able to create the plan that will have all the steps necessary for you to accomplish your goals. Be very precise; do not think any of the steps are obvious. If you think one or more of the steps are obvious, you may not give yourself enough time to achieve your goals and you may not know that you need that extra time. Now complete the next exercise to create your action plan:

Exercise 9: Developing an action plan

Write one of your SMART goals and use it as the title for your action plan. To create it, you will need to think of absolutely everything that you need to do to reach your end target. Probably the list will come with all the steps in chronological order, however, don't worry so much about that. First, think of every task you would need to do. Remember to work on one goal first, and if you feel like it, grab another page and work on your other two goals.

Example:

SMART Goal: I will get all my spelling words correct in the next test.

Action plan:

1. Put together a list of all the spelling words I have learned so far.
2. Study one word per day until I have each word memorised.
3. Ask Dad to test me for the words in order.
4. Ask Mum to test me for the words in random order.

5. Repeat the words I didn't spell correctly and the ones I was not sure about.

SMART Goal #1: ....

Action plan:

1. ....

2. ....

3. ....

4. ....

5. ....

Now go back to the action plan and read each task again. Are they in order? If not, change the number at the front to show the real order in which you must follow them.

After having organised your list, the next step is to assign the dates by which you will complete each task. Remember to keep it realistic. (You cannot study a list of 100 words all in one day.) If you must delegate or ask somebody for help (e.g., Dad to help you with the home test) ask them when they can complete that task. If you realise that your target date for the goal is too soon or too far away, go ahead and change it. Nothing is set in stone! At the end, transfer those tasks and dates to a calendar so you can have it handy for your reference. Always keep that calendar where you can see it every day (e.g., on your desk, on the fridge door, on your closet door, on the bathroom mirror). That way you will not forget about the tasks you have planned, and you will stay on course to achieving your goal. Every morning when you see the calendar, check if you have to set aside some time to complete one or more tasks and you will be on your way to success.

CHAPTER 6:
MINI GOALS

My family lives in Argentina, and we go every year to visit them for Christmas. We always have a wonderful time there with all my cousins, aunts, and of course my mum and dad. The kids love to go because they get entertained and spoiled every day and they have many cousins their own age. But we all dread the flight there. It is such a long trip that there are no direct flights. Depending on the airline we use, we either stop in Auckland, New Zealand or Santiago, Chile.

To make the trip more bearable, if we have time, we may stop for a few days in some fun place such as Disneyland. That way, every time we start the journey to go to Argentina, we look forward not only to arriving there but also to arriving at our mid-destination, because at least we can see that we are much closer to Argentina. When we work on our goals, we may have the same dreadful feeling if it takes too long to achieve the goal, or if it is a very large goal. That is why we create mini goals, or milestones in the middle of our journey, working towards achieving that goal.

There are many reasons why we create milestones. The first one is to have some kind of sign that we are headed in the right direction towards achieving our goal. Another benefit is that by achieving a milestone, we feel the same sense of accomplishment and self-pride as when we achieve the goal. That feeling gives us the motivation and energy we need to continue working towards the goal. And if the goal is too large or difficult, we will definitely need that little push that comes from feeling successful. Can you imagine the happiness and excitement you will feel when you see that you achieve your goals much more quickly than you expected? That joy will bring you an energy that will allow you to face any obstacles to get what you want. And you can get that same joy by creating mini goals or milestones.

As you can see, one thing is to create a mini goal for a large goal, such as learning a list of words to spell that the teacher has given you throughout the whole year. This is a large goal and it could be useful and powerful to create milestones to get the energy and motivation along the way until you achieve the main goal. You could create the milestones by dividing the big list into mini lists of words you learned in each term, or just divide it by an equal number. But if you have a small goal that you can achieve by just following your plan of action, creating milestones would be counterproductive, as it may make you feel disinterested, bored, and basically that this is a total waste of time. You must remember that goals should be realistic but challenging at the same time. They should require an effort from you to achieve them. The fact that milestones are like smaller goals should not make them less challenging.

Thinking of a list of words to learn to spell, if each milestone is a list of 25 words, for example, then that should be challenging enough. But if the milestone is to learn one word and the next milestone is to learn the next word, how boring and long would the process be? And it would also completely take the joy and energy out of the feeling of accomplishment. Let's be realistic; what is the accomplishment in that case? Learning just one word? Big diddly deal. On the other hand, learning 25 words could be something to celebrate. So remember to make your milestones challenging as well, and have them only for a goal that is too large or too far away so you can stay motivated to keep working towards it until the date you set as a target. Let's work on our next exercise to create milestones for your large or long goals.

Exercise 10: Creating milestones

Write one of your large SMART goals and decide whether you could use some milestones in the process to keep you motivated until you reach your main goal. Remember to use your notebook if you need extra space.

Example:

SMART Goal: I will get an A on the final spelling test.

Milestone #1: I will learn how to spell the words learned during term 1.

Milestone #2: I will learn how to spell the words learned during term 2.

Milestone #3: I will learn how to spell the words learned during term 3.

Milestone #4: I will learn how to spell the words learned during term 4.

SMART Goal: ....

Milestone #1: ....

Milestone #2: ....

Milestone #3: ....

Milestone #4: ....

CHAPTER 7: IT'S PARTY TIME! PRESENTS DELIGHT

One thing is sure: every milestone and every goal will challenge you enough to merit a celebration. This is another part of the process that will bring you so much fun: to celebrate when you reach each milestone and goal. It is so necessary, you worked so hard to reach them, so now... PAR-TAY! What do you get at a party? Presents! Because reaching each milestone or goal is like a party, that is what we will get every time it happens: a present for ourselves or a reward. I know, sometimes the reward is the actual goal itself, for example if your goal was to save enough money to buy an Xbox. Here the "present" or reward for reaching the goal is to go to the store and buy the Xbox and start playing with it. With all the other goals, reaching a goal feels like a reward itself, because achieving the goal is something nice that happens to you. (I doubt you created any negative goal, right? "I will get Mum and Dad to take my iPad away because I won't do my chores." Crazy!) But the reality is that you worked very hard to get there. You had some challenges, you went through some other times that you didn't feel like working, or you had to stop yourself from doing something you really wanted to do (buying lollies) and do what was the right thing to do (save the money). So you definitely deserve to have a reward for your hard work.

The main reason to have a reward every time you hit a milestone is to keep you going. A reward will make you feel happy and will remind you of the hard work you did to achieve that milestone. And that happiness will fuel extra energy to keep working towards the main goal. Remember, we create milestones when it takes a long time to achieve a certain goal. In that case, the energy fades and you may want to give up the goal altogether. But if you hit a milestone and the consequence is that you get a little pressie, how much more will you keep fighting to work on the plan to reach your goal? I know if I see that I get a present at the end of an action plan, then I want that present, so I will do whatever is necessary to get it!

How are you going to reward yourself every time you hit a milestone? This is another great time to dream again! It could be anything you want, as long as it exists in the real world and your parents allow it. For example, if you want to jump from an airplane with a parachute, I know this is real, and many people have done it, however, I have serious doubts that Mum and Dad would allow you to do it, right? Or you could decide that you want one million dollars as a reward, which Mum and Dad would happily welcome, but let's be honest, how real is that reward?

To decide what reward you will choose for each milestone, you can think of anything that you would find interesting, or something you really want, or even an activity you like doing. You do not need to spend money to have a reward. For example, one of my favourite activities is to go to a bookstore that also has a café and grab some books and read them by myself while having a nice coffee with a treat. So I book that as a reward for some of my milestones. Another one of my favourite activities is to spend some time lying on the beach when the weather is nice and warm or having a bath with my favourite bath bombs. Even booking a free event at the local library is a great reward for my milestones.

Another way to think of rewards would be to reference the kind of milestone that you are working on. For example, as an author, I set up a goal of writing a certain number of books per year. If I write the amount of words I need to write a month to work on my book, I reward myself with a notebook. As an avid reader, if I finish reading the number of books I need to read in a month to work on my annual target, I reward myself with a book. Regarding my health, if I work out every weekday for a month, I reward myself with some workout clothes. You see, it can be fun and even challenging to think of different rewards that relate to your milestone.

Finally, it could be helpful to have a list of rewards that you can reference every time you need to link a reward to a milestone. Sometimes we cannot come up with any idea for a reward, so it is handy to have a list around if you need one while planning. Keep your list handy, like on your nightstand, so every time you come up with an idea for a reward, you enter it on your list. You never know how or when it can come in useful.

Next you will find another exercise, in which you will grab one goal and its milestones and decide what rewards you want to give yourself when you achieve each of them. If you prefer, and you feel creative, get a list going in your goals notebook with all the rewards you can think of for future milestones and/or goals. As usual, look at my example first so you can get an idea of what to think of.

Exercise 11: Setting up rewards

Write the SMART goal you are working on and each of its milestones. Think of all the different things you would love to have or activities you would love to do that you can assign to each milestone. If the goal you are working on does not have any milestones, you can write a list of rewards you can think of for future milestones. Just remember to make the rewards realistic and approved by your parents.

Example:

SMART Goal: I will pass the audition for the local drama play.

Milestone #1: I learn all the lines for the audition.

Reward: Get a new book.

Milestone #2: I learn to sing the song for the audition.

Reward: Watch the movie The Greatest Show.

Milestone #3: I learn the choreography for the audition.

Reward: Have a playdate with Zoe, my friend from ballet.

SMART Goal: ....

Milestone #1: ....
Reward: ....

Milestone #2: ....
Reward: ....

Milestone #3: ....
Reward: ....

Amazing work! You came up to some great dreams, made them possible to achieve, created some brilliant action plans to make them a reality, and even set up some fab prizes every time you hit a milestone in your journey. I am so proud of you! But most importantly, you should be proud of yourself. You just created something that most people (yes, even adults) have never thought of before: how to make their dreams come true.

In the upcoming chapters we will hit the last part of the book, in which we will talk about other situations that you need to consider if you want your ride to success to be fast but not furious (like the movie? Fast and Furious? Get it?).

PART 4

V.I.S. (Very Important Stuff)

I have good news and bad news for you. Let me start with the bad news so you don't stay too upset for too long. The bad news is that you will encounter some challenges, obstacles, and some not so nice situations on your journey to achieve your goals. Now for the good news: you have the power, control, and weapons within yourself to deal with them and overcome them. Sounds exciting? Maybe risky? I know, perhaps you feel a bit scared. "Me? Power and weapons? Not so nice situations? I'm a Celebrity... Get Me Out of Here!" Yes, I know all about feeling scared; been there, done that. But let me tell you something: even if you decide not to create any goals for yourself and go with the flow, you will still find challenges and not so nice situations. I know you are super smart (you would not be reading this book otherwise!), so how about we think about what those situations might be so we are prepared to attack them from the get-go and get it over with? Let's hear that roar!!

CHAPTER 8: UH-OH! THIS IS GETTING TOUGH

I f there is something I like very much and I am quite proud of, is how well prepared I am in many aspects of my life, especially around the kitchen. It is very rare that I must make an impromptu visit to the store because I have run out of milk or bread or anything. It's so rare that I do remember the few times that this has happened to me. Do you want to know how prepared am I? Let's put it this way: I have not only milk in my fridge but also "emergency" milk in my pantry. I also have "emergency" cream, "emergency" bread in my freezer, some "emergency" leftovers in my freezer as well, and even "emergency" toilet paper! (You don't want to realise one day that you are out of toilet paper at the last minute!) I am so prepared that I am never in a panic to see what I am going to cook for dinner if I haven't been in the supermarket for more than a week. That gives me total peace of mind, so that I am always in a good place and will never be left in the lurch. That is how I want you to feel when it comes to working on your goals. If something happens, if anything gets in the way, if there is any challenge or obstacle, I want you to be prepared, knowing that you will be fine because you have the tools you need to overcome any difficulty that comes your way. And let me be clear: you will have difficulties, obstacles, and problems coming your way.

Ugh! Everything has been so smooth and clear up until now. Why did I have to turn to the depressing route and ruin the fun? Was that necessary? Let me be short and sweet (OK, not sweet). Yes. There is no way to sugar-coat this part of the book: you will face some situations that may make you want to quit your goals. You will be tired, you will get bored, you will think that this is not for you, you will get distracted with other stuff. It will happen. Period. So if it is going to happen no matter what, we had better be prepared, so when that moment arrives, we know what to do.

You may be thinking, "Well, if I didn't have to work on my goals then I wouldn't have to face any of those obstacles you are telling me about!" I am so sorry to burst your bubble: your problems would be even worse if you didn't have any goal to work on or any dream to achieve. The reason is that without a goal that you and only you created, decided, and planned what steps to follow to achieve it, then you would be going with the flow, letting life and others dictate what you are going to do/get/have/be. Pretty easy, you may say. Pretty lazy, I may say. And pretty unpredictable as well. You would not have any control over your own life whatsoever. And when you have no control of your life, troubles and problems come mountain-sized, just because other people and circumstances have decided what you are doing with your life. Not only that, but since you are totally unprepared, you feel that you are on a roller coaster that has no end, and you just want to get off! But hey, somebody or something else is deciding when you get off, because you have not created your own life. And that is not a nice situation to be in.

So enough of the introduction to the troubles and tribulations of the goal-setting sisterhood and brotherhood. Let's now think of anything that we might encounter and how we can deal with it so we can continue on the path towards success.

1. Distractions

The first problem we will deal with is distractions. You know when you are doing your homework and then your dog comes to sniff you and then all of a sudden you are playing ball with him? Or when you are setting the table and there is a funny ad on TV and suddenly you realise you are sitting on the couch watching cartoons? Well, that is the power of distractions. Without you even noticing, you find yourself doing something completely different from what you were supposed to do. You know it is going to happen. It happens to all of us: children, teenagers, and adults. So we have to be prepared.

One way to minimise any distractions is to set up dates in your calendar for any action or step you must follow. That way, if you get distracted while you are working on your goal, as soon as you realise that you are distracted, you can promptly go back to doing what you were doing. Also, just by having a set-up date for each action, you will realise much more rapidly that you are getting distracted or that you are straying off the path that you had set up for yourself. It is like having an alarm clock that wakes you up from la-la-land. The moment you entered that date in your calendar, you also entered it into your subconscious, which creates an automatic shake that will remind you to stay focused. If you really want to achieve that goal, your brain will do whatever is necessary to keep you on track.

2. Lack of Motivation

This obstacle is very similar to the one before about distractions. Lack of motivation, or boredom, comes from not reminding yourself about the main goal and your big "why." Your big why is the main reason you want to achieve your goal. That is what prompted you to create your dream in the first place. It is like a little switch in your heart that makes you get all excited every time you think about it. And that is why you never set up a goal that is not relevant to you and your main interests, likes and passions. Because when you set up a goal that relates to what you are supposed to want, or what you believe your parents or teachers want from you, as opposed to what you deeply want, then your "why" is insignificant. You don't have any excitement when you think about it. You don't jump up and down when you imagine what you would feel having achieved the goal. And without excitement and motivation, you may one day want to give up altogether, because you are bored, or have found some challenges, or because something you are really interested in came your way.

So if you ever feel like you are losing your excitement about the goal, or if you don't feel like working on it, go back to the notebook where you are working, or the exercise at the beginning of the book when you were creating all your dreams. Look at the dream that relates to that goal you have not been feeling like working on lately. Visualise living the dream, having achieved it. How does it feel? Are you happy? Excited? Over the moon and stars? That is a great feeling and it will help you remember what your big why is and keep you committed and motivated to continue working on making it a reality.

3. Lack of Time

This is a very interesting obstacle, because it may happen for many reasons. On one hand, it could happen because other things appear in your life, little situations that you did not consider when you decided on your action plan. It could be some extra homework that you have to do, or suddenly you went on a holiday to the country for a week, or perhaps the day that you needed to take a certain step in your action plan you had a big fight with your brother and that made you upset and wasted your time. Or sometimes the situations that appear in your life are not really little, but so big that they end up being ginormous, like if your goal was to win one game at your school athletics carnival and two weeks prior, you had a big fall and fractured your leg. What are the odds! But the reality is that those situations may happen, because that is the way life works, and life happens. And it may take us completely off track. In some other cases, the reason we find ourselves with very little time to reach our goal is because we may have set up a wrong deadline. You might not have calculated correctly the time you needed to go through the action plan and the target date is here and you still haven't done everything necessary to achieve your goal, even though you worked really hard without getting distracted. No matter what the reason is, the solution is very simple: move your target date.

There is a very smart and highly successful personal and business consultant called Brian Tracy, and he trains adults on how to set up goals. And one thing he always says is that if you write a proper SMART goal, there is no such thing as a wrong goal, just a wrong target date. That means that you may have to move your target date to a later date when those little or big situations appear in your life. But keep working on it, and, for sure, you will find success. Just remember that sometimes little things appear that we allow to appear, such as playing on the Xbox for too long, or watching TV all day, and we end up wasting time. If something like that happens, you can absolutely control that, so call them distractions and refer to point 1. That is why you always must ask yourself: am I on track? Is what I am doing a time waster or something that needs to be done? If you can control it and it is not urgent and important, remove it, move on, and keep working. If you cannot control it or it is something that is urgent and important, then go back to your notebook and your calendar and review your dates.

4. Fear

Such a short word, with such an ugly meaning. This is the original F word, very powerful and super negative at the same time. There are many fears, and we all have many, a few, one or all of them. There is fear of failure, fear of success, fear of rejection, fear of the unknown, the trendy FOMO or fear of missing out, fear of being alone, and many others. But no matter what kind of fear it is, the consequences can be from inconvenient to severely damaging. And I don't mean the consequences of acting on this fear. Quite the opposite; it would be the consequence of avoiding what causes the fear. That is what most people, children, and adults, usually do. They avoid the situations that could cause them the fear, so for the short term they feel safe and comfortable. But staying in your comfort zone creates a paralysis that will make you stay just the way you are and never develop or grow, and certainly, never achieve any goal, because it is not possible to stay in your comfort zone and achieve something challenging at the same time.

We have learned already that to achieve any goal, to make any dream a reality, we must work, and work really hard. But if you fear that you will do something wrong, or that you will be rejected for being successful, you end up getting stuck, and something called *procrastination* makes its way into the play. Procrastination is something that appears to almost all of us, and it means that we delay doing what we must do because of excuses we make up. For example, I need to fold the laundry, but I will procrastinate and leave it for later because I really hate folding laundry. So, I will find other things that are more interesting for me to do before doing that. And all of a sudden, a whole week went by, the clothes are dry already and have been in a pile for that whole time. And what is worse, none of us have anything to wear because they are all in the laundry room waiting for me to fold them and put them in each closet.

I suffer from this too. I understand procrastination very well, because I am very guilty of it. The difference with my younger self is that now I am aware when I am procrastinating and can discover right away the real reason for it. And actually, the laundry example is not something I usually procrastinate about. You know the times I do procrastinate? When I write for this or any other book, many times I have ended up not writing "because I don't have time today, I have to run some errands, complete some spreadsheets, or take the kids to their activities." Or another day, "I am too tired to write, so nothing good will come into the book if I force myself to write." But now I know that those are excuses, because if I decide to sit at the computer for just ten minutes, I realise that I can write many words and fulfil my daily activity to achieve my goal of publishing the book.

So when I find myself making excuses, I stop and ask myself "Why am I making excuses? What is the real reason why I don't want to write?'" Usually it is because I am afraid that I will write something silly or that it will be the wrong thing to write. Sometimes it is because I am almost finished with the book and then I have to find a publisher that likes it. (But they may reject it first, so that would be my fear of rejection working at its best.) But if I end up giving in and the fear wins, nothing gets done. I would never know if I would fail or not unless I tried. That is why I push myself to overcome the procrastination, put the excuse to the side, and make things happen. And they end up happening! Next time you find yourself making excuses for why you cannot follow your action plan, ask yourself if that is just an excuse, if you could overcome it somehow, and think about why you are making excuses. What do you fear? Is it rejection? Failure? Making a mistake? No matter what the fear is, overcome the excuse that you are using by doing something, even something little that is opposite to that excuse, and you will see that procrastination ends up being just a weird word and fear just a short word.

5. Too Many Goals

One thing I mentioned in the first few exercises is that you may have many, if not hundreds, of dreams to make come true, but it is better to work on only a few at a time; even one would be great. When we have too many goals to work on, we end up feeling overwhelmed about the amount of work we must do, so we may do nothing at all. Also since you are working on so many things at the same time, you can dedicate only a little amount of time to each of them, and end up not seeing much progress, which leads to frustration, which leads to giving up.

This one is easy: start by creating one to three goals. If it is your first experience of setting goals, have only one, to get a grip on what it requires you to do. As you become more knowledgeable about how to work on each plan, you can add goals. But I feel that three should be the maximum you should work on at any given time. Don't worry about that huge list of dreams you wrote at the beginning – the dreams are still there, so you can always work on them as you finish working on your first goals. Also, sometimes it may happen that as time goes by, your dreams change. (Today you are all about Barbies, and tomorrow you only want to play with your LEGO®.) It is okay for dreams to change. They may not change as quickly as just mentioned, but you should not force yourself to keep dreams that are no longer interesting (and relevant) for you. Just remember to work on your main one to three goals at a time, and when you achieve one, you can move on to the next one on your list.

6. No Improvement For A While

How frustrating would it be to work like a maniac for your

goal, practicing every day and not seeing any improvement? I remember when I was working on my running training for a while, before taking part in City2Surf, and I noticed some great improvement, and then one day I realised that I had stopped improving. My speed was the same, my technique was as flawed as it was the week before, and I was not increasing the distance I was running without stopping. I was very disillusioned. I remember thinking, "I am dying here running for so long. Every. Single. Day. And nothing." Sad face. Thoughts of giving up started appearing in my head. But I remembered my father used to tell me: "Life is like an ocean. Sometimes the tide is in, and sometimes the tide is out. No matter what, keep working, because, like in the ocean, both tides will pass." And that kept me going until I started seeing improvement again.

While we are working on our goals, sometimes we are doing great, sometimes we are doing not so great (we are not perfect, right?), and other times, nothing is happening. At all. But keep working, because these nothing boring periods with no results don't last long, and then you will be back at the top of the wave. Happy face!

Exercise 12: Preparing yourself for challenges

Go through the list of your goals, milestones, and action plans, and think of all the challenges and setbacks that you may encounter throughout the process. Then write the challenge/s and think of ways that you could overcome or solve the situation when it arises. Note that some goals or activities may have only one challenge, but sometimes you may find more than one challenge to overcome. The same will happen with the solutions. Sometimes we may find more than one solution for each challenge. If you notice in the following examples, the first goal has two challenges with one solution each, and the second goal has only one challenge but two solutions for it!

Example #1:

Goal: I learn all my timetables by memory by the end of Term 2.

Challenge #1: I don't have enough time to practise.

Solution: I will dedicate 15 minutes after school every Monday and Thursday to practise.

Challenge #2: I may get bored after a while.

Solution: Create different games to practise, like using songs to learn each table or write them down, using as many colours as I can.

Example #2:

Goal: I save $100 to buy Barbie Airplane before my birthday.

Challenge #1: I also want to use the money for lollies.

Solution: Create a Lollie Jar to put part of the money I get in, and the rest goes to the Barbie Airplane Jar.

Challenge #2: I feel it will take too long to save that money, so I will give up.

Solution #1: Look for a picture of the Barbie Airplane online and put it in my bedroom so I can remember my goal every day.

Solution #2: Offer to do more chores around the house to get more money.

Next you will find enough space to complete challenges and

solutions for one goal. Grab your goals notebook and repeat the exercise for the rest of your goals.

Goal #1: ....

Challenge #1: ....

Solution #1: ....

Solution #2: ....

Solution #3: ....

Challenge #2: ....

Solution #1: ....

Solution #2: ....

Solution #3: ....

We just went through a list of challenges and obstacles that we will (and I repeat: WILL) encounter on our journey to goal achievement, and we talked about some ways to overcome them. In the next chapter, we will talk about what habits we can create that will help us immensely with our journey and what habits to replace. Stay tuned!

CHAPTER 9: HAPPITS

When we talk about goals, and dreams, and the future, it all seems like a galaxy far, far away. We start imagining "some day when I achieve my goals, I will be a different person. I will be happier, successful, and full of energy". It will be *The Future*. How cool does that look? How different will you be? How much happier? Newsflash: You start constructing your future *today*. NOW. What you are doing at this very moment will determine how your future will develop. What? That's a bit much, isn't it? Well, not really. The things we do every day will end up creating our future. That is why we have to be very careful about what we decide to do every day. For example, if every day you play video games and forget about reading, or doing homework, most probably your grades will suffer. If every day you come home and go straight to your bedroom without even talking to your mum, most probably you won't have a very close relationship with her. If every day you go to bed and you wake up and do not brush your teeth, most probably you will have dental problems and will have to visit a dentist often, your teeth may hurt and may be smelly and yellow. On the other hand, if every evening you take a shower, you will sleep deeper and longer, and the next day you will smell fresh and clean. If every day you take some time to practise your reading and spelling, you will be able to read and write more complex pieces and you will enjoy more the time doing it because it will be effortless.

What is it we must continually do to create the future we want (that is, to achieve our goals and be happy)? It is called habits. That is the behaviour or activity you do repeatedly, so often that it becomes automatic for you. You do not even have to think about doing it; you do not have to force yourself to do it; you do not have to have any willpower. It is just part of you, and you just do it. And the days you don't do it for whatever reason (you are sick, you just got a little brother and are visiting Mum at the hospital, you are in another country and you don't have what you need around you), you feel uncomfortable because you are not doing it. What happens when your activity pops up automatically is that the excuses do not even come into your head. You do not even contemplate making an excuse. It's the same thing if you feel uncomfortable about not doing it: you will do whatever is necessary to follow through the activity or action that you had planned. If you follow through, and you don't even have to think about it or force yourself to do it, you are on the path to achieving success.

The other benefit of creating a habit that leads you to success is that while you are following through, you are already experiencing the happiness that you will feel when you achieve that goal. The reason is that your brain will know that you are advancing towards it, that you are doing something that will cause you to achieve that goal. That will trigger you to experience the satisfaction of doing something right, you will feel better about yourself, and it will make you feel happy. That is why I call them *"happits"* instead of *"habits"*, because that repetition will give you a sense of happiness that you may not feel just by repeating a random behaviour.

The formula is:

$$ACTIVITY \times REPETITION = HABIT$$

$$HABIT + HAPPY = HAPPIT$$

$$HAPPIT + GOAL = SUCCESS$$

After considering and understanding the importance of creating *happits,* let's talk about the method to create one. You may think it is just as easy as saying, "From now on, I will practise my spelling for 10 minutes every day). Yyyyeeeaaaahhh......nah. Sorry. Nothing is that easy. If it were that easy, we would all be super successful, have all the time in the world to have fun, and nothing would take too much effort. The method to create a happit is both simple and difficult at the same time. I will give you a few tips that will help you:

1. Stay On It

Think about your pet, or any pet you can imagine. How do dogs get trained? Usually the trainer gives them a reward in the form of a snack and/or praise every time the dog does what the trainer is telling it to do. No, don't worry, I am not suggesting that you treat yourself like a puppy, or that you get candy every time you do what you are supposed to do. (That would be crazy!) What I am suggesting here is that you stay consistent. If you want to form a habit to practise your spelling every day for 10 minutes, set an alarm for the same time every day and follow that prompt to do your practice. If you stay consistent for at least 30 days, you will see results. Some habits require a little more time. If it is something difficult to automatise, maybe you need 60 days (no more than that, I promise). But some other ones, especially the ones you really enjoy, may take as little as a couple of weeks to automatise, and there you have a habit that now you cannot let go.

2. Set Reminders

One problem of not having that habit created already is that, since it does not appear automatically in our heads, then of course we tend to forget to activate it! Funny, right? Most probably you would say "frustrating." It is like buying some vitamins to have with breakfast every day and never opening the jar. Then how do you solve this challenge? Just set reminders! Get some post-it notes and write the habit that you are trying to create and then post it on your mirror, or on the nightstand, or even in your lunch box. (Why not? You have to eat every day, so for sure you will see those little post-it notes.) It will help you to stay consistent until you have it so internalised that you will not need the post-it note anymore. Just remember to keep it for at least 30 days so it becomes automatic.

3. Create Mini Habits

I just love this tip. It is one of my favourites to overcome procrastination. Let me explain what a mini habit is. Sometimes to achieve a goal we need to create a habit that seems so huge that we may feel overwhelmed or scared, and we end up not even trying. Or sometimes the thought of having to do it every day brings us tears of boredom, and again, we end up not even trying. For example, I know I have to take my dog Heidi for a walk every day. And every day I look at her, thinking, "Ugh! I must get her leash and her poopy bags and take her for a 15-minute walk, pick up the poopy, look for a trash bin, then walk all the way back home. What a hassle!" That kind of thinking makes me want to stay home and not do anything. But what if instead of thinking that, I just think "I will grab the leash, the poopy bag, and the dog and open the door"? That is much easier to do, isn't it? What happens is that after having already accomplished this task, I might as well go out and start walking! Then, by the magic of shortening my thinking, I end up doing the whole thing.

Let me tell you, I started using that technique with my other habits and it worked wonders! For example, I am at this very moment using this technique writing this book. If my habit was to write a chapter of my books every day, it would feel too much for me, and many days I would not have the time to accomplish this, so most probably I would fail most of the days, and I would not create a habit because of lack of repetition. To avoid this feeling, I created a mini habit that I can accomplish consistently. My mini habit is to work on my book for about 10 minutes every day. 10 minutes is a very short period of time, so it does not feel overwhelming to me. Even when I have a very busy day I usually can find 10 minutes to work on my book. Even if I don't feel inspired, something comes in just 10 minutes. And you know what happens? Many times I end up working for longer than 10 minutes. Just because the habit was tiny enough that I didn't feel scared or nervous or overwhelmed about doing it. It just felt simple and quick. You can use the same technique with your own habits. You will see magic happening!

4. Replace Bad Habits

One problem about being comfortable is that we keep some

habits we know are not good for us, just because it is difficult to get rid of them. If it were not comfortable for us to keep them, it would not be difficult to get rid of those bad habits. You know what I am talking about: watching too many YouTube videos, playing Minecraft for too long, not eating our vegetables, not waking up at the right time so we avoid having to rush to arrive at school on time. Etcetera. Etcetera. Oh, yes! Etcetera.

The problem with bad habits is that they take our energy and motivation to do what is best to accomplish our goals. Sometimes they can even ruin our chances to accomplish those goals. For example, let's say your goal is to convert the largest number of tries in every rugby game this year and become the Player of the Match in your team. If you stay up late every night before the game because you want to play Minecraft, then you will be beyond tired during the game the next day. Not only you will not score any try, your coach may not want to give you the chance to play because you look so tired. Then you see that bad habit ruined your opportunity to accomplish your goal. On the other hand, sometimes the consequence a bad habit can have on your goal journey may not be that obvious. For example, if your goal is to get a Principal's Award for your commitment to school, but you are always rushing because you wake up too late, then it is possible that you may end up arriving late at school some days (too much traffic, you forgot your lunch box, your little baby brother just got his nappy very dirty and your mum had to change him). If you arrive late sometimes, the principal may think that you are not that committed to school. As a result, you may not get that award you want so much.

But don't beat yourself up! And don't be ashamed either. We all carry bad habits. Some of us try to overcome them, and others don't. What side are you on? After learning about how damaging bad habits can be in the pursuit of your goals, it is time to determine how to get rid of them. And once again, I have bad news and good news for you. The bad news is that you cannot get rid of them. Yep, sorry, there is no such thing as saying, "From now on I will wake up earlier and that is it." Because after a few days of fighting and pushing hard to make it happen, you will get tired, or fed up, and that is it. You will sleep in and throw everything into the garbage.

On the other hand, there are some good news: the way to solve this problem is by replacing bad habits with new ones (not bad, for sure!). What you must do is to think what new habit can replace the bad one and have the same feeling you had before. For example, if your bad habit is to sleep in in the mornings so you can feel more rested, your new habit could be to go to bed a bit earlier so you can sleep the same amount of time you slept before. Or if your bad habit is to watch videos for too long instead of doing your homework, your new habit could be to do your homework first, get it out of the way, so you have time to watch videos with no guilt and anxiety about not having your homework done. In any case, it is just a matter of sitting down and deciding what habits you currently have that are helpful to achieve your goals (and keep them) and which ones are negative and would hurt your chances to achieve your goals, and replace them with helpful ones.

Exercise 13: New Happits

List of all your current habits that are not beneficial for you or your goals and think of all the ways you can replace them. Also add any mini habit you can think of that could help you, and the reminders to keep you on track.

Example

Goal	Habit to replace	New Habit	Mini Habit	Reminder
Arrive at school on time every day this year	Waking up too late	Go to bed half an hour earlier	Start with 5 minutes earlier and increase by 5 minutes every other day until half an hour	Set an alarm for bedtime in my Chromebook.
Win the reading competition at school	Playing Minecraft too much after dinner every night	Read at least 10 minutes every night in bed	Go to bed 10 minutes earlier and have a book ready on my nightstand	Leave a post-it note with the reading level on my computer for me to see every time I play Minecraft

Sometimes you may have more than one habit to replace, or you may not have any bad habit and just want to create a good habit to help you achieve your goals.

Complete the exercise in the next page and continue in your goals notebook if you need more space.

Goal	Habit to replace	New Habit	Mini Habit	Reminder

CHAPTER 10: NOW FOR SOME OTHER VERY IMPORTANT SUPPORT SYSTEMS

We all need help. That is how life works. As human beings, we are very similar to the way some animals behave: we need the troop to hang out with to help and be helped. (And considering that humans evolved from monkeys, it makes sense, right?) Sometimes the help will come from other monkeys people, sometimes it will come from visuals, other times will come just from being relaxed and having a little silence. But no matter what, we all can use some help and support to achieve our goals much faster and more efficiently. These are some of the most popular ones:

1. Good Ol' Friends and Family

There is an old song called "With a Little Help from My Friends." And when I say old, I mean super old, like ancient, as it was created before your mum and dad were even born! But I think it is relevant today, because it talks about how we get by and want to try new things with some help from our friends. Because a long (LOOOOOOONG) time ago people needed help and support to achieve what they wanted. Today we all need help and support to achieve what we want. And in the future, when we can tele-transport ourselves to another part of the world just by thinking about it, we will still need help and support to achieve what we want. Why? Because we human beings are social entities. We cannot survive on our own. So why do we think we can achieve every single dream and goal we have just by ourselves?

The main support we can get to achieve our goals is from people around us. If we let our family and friends know about our goals, I promise you, they will want to help you achieve them, so if they can help you in any way, they will. For example, Dad can remind us every morning about our goal when we have a little difficulty waking up on time. And our friend from gymnastics can remind us of our goal of learning to do the cartwheel when we feel like not going to gymnastics class. How about our goal to learn to speak Mandarin Chinese? If you tell the teacher about it, I am sure she would be thrilled to give you a little book she found to help you. People can help us to achieve our goals in many ways, by giving us support and by keeping us accountable, so we can always focus on our target.

Exercise 14: Looking for somebody to help

Think of everybody that you can ask for help for every action, habit, or challenge you can think of:

Example:

1. Mum

2. Dad

3. Teacher

4. Coach

5. Grandma and Grandpa

6. Auntie

7. Best Friend

1. ....

2. ....

3. ....

4. ....

5. ....

6. ....

7. ....

8. ....

9. ....

2. Dear Diary

I love this support system. I have been using it since I first learned how to read and write. I got my first journal at six years old, and since that day, I have never stopped writing in a journal. I have used it to write about my experiences, my daily adventures (and misadventures), my thoughts, my opinions, my happy times and sad times. No matter what I wrote about, I felt that writing was giving me clarity to understand my emotions, my desires, and, best of all, myself. Nowadays, I enjoy starting my day writing in my journal. I can talk about what I am grateful for, what I need to improve, or where to focus my energy that day. For example, if I have two or three goals that I am working on at the same time, I can decide that day that I will focus my energy on one of them be-cause I have practice time that will help me with it. Or perhaps my focus will be on improving my productivity that day and avoiding distractions so I can work on aspects of each of the goals. Or I can write about something great that happened the day before, or how great the day will be so I can start on a very positive note. I also like to write about any thought or idea that I come up with after waking up, since while sleeping all night, my brain had a chance to engage all its creativity without interruptions or distractions. Per-haps you woke up with an idea that will increase your chances of achieving your goal, or some new activity that if you add to your action plan, it will benefit the process for achieving your goal. The idea for a journal is that it will give you clarity and motivation to keep working on your goals.

Exercise 15: Creating My First Journal

This one is easy, and you should be able to do it in a very short time. Grab one of your notebooks (one of many, if you are like my daughter Emma) and write the title: "Diary of Ideas, Thoughts, and Data to Achieve my Goals" on the first page. This will be your first journal.

3. Affirmations

Affirmations are just sentences that will enhance your self-confidence and your belief that you have what is necessary to achieve your goals. Think about the way you talk to your BFF when she has a concern. Let's say you invite your BFF over for some bike riding, but she feels a bit scared because she fell off a while ago and is worried that she may hurt herself again. What would you say to her? Would you say, "Silly girl! You will never learn how to ride the bike!" I'm sure you wouldn't. It would not be very nice to treat your friend that way, and it would not be very helpful for her to overcome that fear, right? Most probably you would say something like, "Come on, you can do it! I know you will ride well, and you will enjoy it". Now instead of thinking of your friend, let's say it is you that wants to ride your new bike, but you are a bit scared. What would you say to yourself? Would you say, "Come on! You can do it!" or would you say, "Silly me!" If you talk to your BFF so nicely so she can overcome her fear, why wouldn't you talk to yourself the same way? Affirmations help you with that. By creating "cheering" statements to yourself, you are not only motivating yourself to continue trying but also programming your mind that you have all that is necessary for you to succeed, and that you are good enough, you deserve to achieve your goal.

I absolutely use affirmations every morning, and they have helped me over the years to develop my self-confidence and self-esteem. Some affirmations are about the goal already achieved ("I do perfect cartwheels in gymnastics" or "I have read two full books this month") and some affirmations are about yourself while working on achieving your goal ("I wake up every day at 7 AM to have enough time to prepare for school" or "I am focused on finishing my school activities on time"). I like these kinds of affirmations very much because I feel that I can relate better to them, as they form part of my daily life. The way to use affirmations is by creating them and then you can either say them aloud or write them down. Either way will help your mind to get the idea and internalise it completely. It may sound ridiculous at the beginning, but if you persevere and keep using them, you will become accustomed to them and won't feel awkward anymore, and, what's best, you will see the results after a while of using them.

Exercise 16: Affirmations Galore

Think of all the affirmations that can help you programme your "computer brain" to set yourself up for success. You can keep them in your journal or on a wall in your bedroom so you can see them every day.

Examples:

* I have all the energy, determination, and strength inside me to achieve all my goals.

* I deserve to succeed in my life.

* I am brave and confident.

* Never give up!

Your Affirmations:

1. ....

2. ....

3. ....

4. ....

5. ....

4. I Spy, With My Little Eyes, Something Beginning With...

"...my goals!" This support system is called Vision Board, and it is actually super fun. It involves making a collage with pictures that describe or show your goals already achieved. The success of this system is that it works with the fact that the brain does not differentiate an image of something real from an image of some-thing that has not happened yet. If you see the picture of your goal already achieved, your brain will do whatever is necessary to restore the balance and bring your reality to that image. For ex-ample, if you are learning to play golf and want to improve (and maybe even win a game against Dad), you can look at a picture of a great golf player and imagine it is you. Or you could, for example, look at a picture of Tiger Woods hitting the ball when he was your age. That way you can imagine it is you winning, and your brain will focus and put all your energy into bringing that image to life. This is so much fun that you will want to do it even if it is your time to play Minecraft!

Start by having all your goals in front of you. Get a tablet or laptop and Google some of the main words of the goal, then click on "Images." Print the best images you can find that you can identify with or that can best represent you having achieved that goal. If your parents allow you to have social media, maybe create a Pinterest account (private would be best) with the pictures you choose. You can also add some of the affirmations you created before, or you can look for quotes that will help you along the way. You can write them down on little pieces of paper or print them if you found them on a website. Afterwards, cut them out and place them on a big piece of paper, something that you could hang in your bedroom and see every night before you sleep and every morning when you wake up. Or you could get a whiteboard and place all your pictures on it with magnets. But you have to look at your board every day to increase your chances to achieve your goals. Don't worry, it is your own Vision Board, so if you feel that you need to change some images because they don't work too well, or you need to add or take off some quotes because it is too messy, you can do it! You could also draw some images or anything that could make your board more attractive. It is YOUR Vision Board, remember? You can do whatever you want with it, as long as you look at it every day.

Exercise 17: Creating My Vision Board

Write all the keywords you want to use for your Google search for images. Then enter your words and look for all the images you want to print. Grab a piece of cardboard, a whiteboard or canvas and place all your pictures on it. You can write some quotes

or your affirmations and draw or paint to decorate your Vision
Board, even place some stickers or jewels on it if you want. Have
fun!

Examples of keywords:

* Barbie Made-To-Move (or the toy you are saving your money
to buy).

* Swimming (or the sport you want to excel at).

* Bycicle

* Art Supplies

* Drama

Examples of Quotes

"Why fit in when you were born to stand out?"   *Dr Seuss*

"Always do the thing you think you cannot do." *Eleanor
Roosevelt*

"Make each day your masterpiece." *John Wooden*

"No one is perfect. That's why pencils have erasers."   *Wolf-
gang Riebe*

*"Yesterday is history. Tomorrow is a mystery. Today is
a gift. That's why we call it 'The Present.'"* - *Eleanor
Roosevelt*

Your Own Keywords:

1. ....

2. ....

3. ....

4. ....

5. ....

Your Chosen Quotes:

1. ....

2. ....

3. ....

4. ....

5. ....

There you have some of the most useful support systems that you can get your hands on to help you in the process to achieve your goals. You can use one, two, or all of them. I love using the last three as a combination in the morning along with meditation and reading, right before preparing my agenda of what I will do during the day. (Yes, I wake up super early every day.) The idea is to plan your day with your goals in mind and have all these support systems to make that process more efficient. Preparing these support systems is a good investment of time, since just the few minutes that you dedicate to each one will give you the help to achieve all your goals.

CONCLUSION

Do you think you have done enough dreaming and imagining while reading this book? Do you think your plan is efficient enough to make your dreams a reality? I hope you can realise that you are good enough to become whatever you want to be, that you don't need fairy godmothers, genies, or unicorns and rainbows to make your dreams come true. I know you have in you all the strength, determination, and positive energy you need to realise those dreams. Now that you know who you want to be, you could transform your dreams into goals. Having a strategic action plan with relevant activities that you can follow every day until you achieve your goal will give you the comfort of not having to make last-minute decisions on what to do. Knowing prior to encountering any challenges what those challenges can be and how to deal with them will give you the weapons to get rid of any "weed in your garden," all while using as many tools, resources and support systems as you can, so you can achieve your goals in a more efficient way.

Dreams can be magic, only if they remain a dream. But when we transform them into goals, there is nothing magic or mysterious about them. They are just a reality waiting to happen.

ACKNOWLEDGMENTS

This book was the best thing I did not know that I had to write. I wrote it for my kids, your kids, and everybody that was a kid at some point. It was not an easy task, but with the help of many people the task was finished, and another goal was achieved.

I will be forever grateful to Jacquie Limb, whose creativity and talent made possible a fabulous cover that explains without words all the dreams and goals we have inside to make a reality.

I also want to thank my friends and family and everybody that took the time to read this book and give me some feedback. You not only gave me your testimonial; you also gave me the courage and self-confidence to continue working and believing in myself.

To all the hundreds (or thousands) of authors I have read their books about self-development and growth. You opened my eyes to something much bigger than myself: my legacy.

Finally, I want to thank my family: my loving husband Scott for his continuous support, and my beautiful children, Emma and Luca, because they taught me to see the world through their selfless eyes.

ABOUT THE AUTHOR

Mariana Leader

Mariana Leader is a noted public speaker and corporate trainer who has facilitated public speaking and technology presenting workshops around the globe for companies such as Google, Microsoft, IBM and many other leading firms. After researching and being laser focused on goal generation, Mariana has achieved many of her own life goals. These include studying Marketing and Organisational Management and graduating with honors, starting a business, traveling to over 40 countries, speaking 4 languages, and having a beautiful family and kids. She has also achieved many of her yearly goals such as reading 30 books a year and creating healthy habits such as daily meditation and exercise. And now she has achieved a wonderful new goal: writing a book to inspire as many children as possible to make their dreams a reality.

PRAISE FOR AUTHOR

"Dream4Real is an inspirational book that introduces children to the world of goals and taking action. Through the reading and exercises in this inspiring book, children will be guided to make their dreams a reality!"

- HAL ELROD, INTERNATIONAL KEYNOTE SPEAKER AND BEST-SELLING AUTHOR OF THE MIRACLE MORNING AND THE MIRACLE EQUATION

"Dream4Real is an enjoyable and inspiring book that all children in the world should have the opportunity to read to encourage and guide their dreams. The author makes this beautiful book an easy engaging book that children can read and relate to and most importantly enjoy for many years."

- MADONNA LEWIS - MOTHER OF 4

"We all want to achieve our goals and help those we care about do the same. This brilliant and insightful book gives an excellent step-by-step process for doing just that."

- ZACHARY LEWIS - STUDENT

www.ingramcontent.com/pod-product-compliance
Lightning Source LLC
Chambersburg PA
CBHW060949040426
42445CB00011B/1070